VERANDA

decorating

A sitting area in a Napa Valley retreat by Richard Hallberg is a subtle interplay of rich textures, sculptural furnishings, and an eclectic array of accessories.

VERANDA
decorating

MARIO LOPEZ-CÓRDERO

FOREWORD BY CLINTON SMITH

HEARST
books

Introduction
page 7

F fireplaces, floors, floor lamps
page 61

G gallery walls
page 75

H hallways
page 79

I ikat
page 83

J juxtaposition
page 85

P painted furniture, passementerie, patina, pattern, pendants
page 121

Q quiet
page 135

R ranges, romance, rugs
page 141

S sconces, screens, sisal, slipcovers, staircases, symmetry
page 149

T texture, tiles, toile
page 177

Z zen
page 217

Photography Credits
—page 220

Index
—page 222

A animal prints, antiques, art, art of arrival
page 9

B bathtubs, beds
page 25

C chandeliers, chintz, curtains
page 37

D daybeds, dining rooms, door knockers
page 49

E enfilades
page 57

K kitchens
page 87

L lacquer, libraries, living rooms
page 97

M marble, mirrors
page 107

N nailheads
page 115

O outdoor rooms
page 117

U upholstery
page 187

V vanities, vintage
page 191

W wallcoverigs, wicker, windows
page 199

X x marks the spot
page 211

Y yin & yang
page 215

tents

A new Greek Revival–style house by Amelia Handegan in South Carolina is airy and gracious, thanks to refined antiques and charming architectural details like moldings and chair rails.

Editing a decorating magazine, especially one like *Veranda,* is in many ways the highest kind of education. It's an incomparable perch from which you get to see the best the field has to offer. There are the serene oases in which every yard of linen, every plush seat back, every gracefully placed chalky lamp seems calibrated to take you far, far away. Or the intensely personal tours-de-force that dazzle you with leopard-print needlepoint, chinoiserie pelmets, lacquerwalls so slick that they reflect your face back at you like a mirror—and you can see yourself grinning from ear to ear with the dizzying deliciousness of it all. And then there are the gorgeous and beautiful iterations that fall somewhere in between, homes that split the difference between fireworks and poetry to land on something that reads like a biography and sends you on your way thinking that, yes, maybe you should try marble door casings, or mixing ikat with stripes, or lining your living room in loden green velvet, or hanging curtains with swags, or painting every room white . . . I could go on and on, but I don't have to, because all those lessons are here on these pages and they're our gift to you. Happy decorating.

—Clinton Smith

In an Atlanta living room by Melanie Turner, a sofa covered in tiger-stripe velvet was inspired by one owned by Lee Radziwill and becomes a fittingly stylish and bold focal point.

A animal prints

A who's who of tastemakers have sworn by them, including no lesser personages than the Empress Joséphine, Elsie de Wolfe, Billy Baldwin, Bill Blass, and Albert Hadley, just to name a very few. There's a good reason they're all devotees. When it comes to giving a room a dash of cosmopolitan glamour, nothing does it quite like an animal print. If you're the cautious type, you might want to be judicious in your application—a leopard seat cushion or throw pillow is the chic equivalent of a quiet purr. But there's nothing wrong with a full-throated embrace of the style: an antelope, zebra, or tiger rug lays a versatile, genre-defying foundation for a statement space that's as gutsy as a roar. Welcome to the jungle.

antiques

There is a noble beauty that comes from an armchair or table that has stood the test of time for *centuries*. A gracefully aged, lovingly used antique gives a space a sense of history and a lasting soulfulness that no shiny, fresh-off-the-line piece of furniture ever can. An heirloom can be like an old friend who was there when your great-grandmother took tea and is still hanging around the living room to watch you sip your double macchiato. This points to the important thing to remember with inherited (or seemingly inherited) objects: they must adapt. Nobody wants to live in a museum. Period pieces don't have to dictate period rooms. Think of it as a balancing act. Match a Georgian chest of drawers with a vivid work of contemporary art. Pair a walnut claw-and-ball-footed highboy with diaphanous taffeta curtains and pretty painted floors. The gorgeous results will combine a healthy respect for the past with a joyful celebration of the way we live today.

A nineteenth-century shield-back chair from John Rosselli Antiques has a noble profile and the graceful marks of patina.

left: Ann Getty combines eighteenth-century English gilt armchairs, a Louis XIV table, and Chinese silk panels with an Orientalist work by Jacques-Émile Blanche in her San Francisco home. below: In a pared-down Atlanta living room by D. Stanley Dixon and Carolyn Malone, a neoclassical chest and gilt mirror feel soulfully clean-lined. opposite: Cultures converge in Amelia Handegan's Charleston bedroom, with a nineteenth-century Anglo-Indian desk, a nineteenth-century English armchair, and an antique Indian *pichhwai* wall hanging.

Antiques can adapt. *Period pieces* don't have to dictate period rooms. Nobody wants to live in a museum.

left: A painting by Jeff Perrott dominates a serene New England living room by Richard Hallberg. below: Cheryl Skoog Tague's New York foyer features a grouping of works by William Kelly. opposite: In a Nashville house by Suzanne Kasler, a mist-hued custom wallpaper by Gracie augments an abstract by Steven Seinberg.

art

If a picture is worth a thousand words, then a well-curated space speaks volumes—about history, about culture, about the personalities of the people who live there. In one fell swoop, you can communicate everything you need to say without ever uttering a word. Placement is key. If you want that vibrant, monolithic abstract to be the major note in a room, then set it off with furnishings and fabrics in soft neutrals. A quieter approach might pair a soothing painting with bare walls in a similar, serene shade. And don't ignore the value of matting or a frame. With the right setup, a toddler's imaginative scribbles can achieve the visual impact of a Lichtenstein and serve as a heartfelt, lasting memento to boot.

from left: A niche frames a striking painting by Roy Lichtenstein in a Southampton, New York, house by David Kleinberg. / Also in Southampton, Quinn Pofahl and Jaime Jiménez defy convention by placing a console in front of a floor-to-ceiling abstract by Michael Lee.

from left: Gilt antiques are juxtaposed with a stark contemporary piece in an Atlanta dining room by John Oetgen. / J. Randall Powers achieves the same frisson with an eighteenth-century French chest of drawers, a Michael Taylor chair, and an abstract by Sherie' Franssen in Houston.

A Toronto salon by Jan Showers has the hushed atmosphere of a gallery and doubles as an entertaining space; the artworks are by Jason Salavon.

art of arrival

It's as true in decoration as it is in life: you never get a second chance to make a good first impression. Start in the driveway and think of the curb appeal. Does your façade beckon visitors with an inviting garden, a lacquered front door, the crunch of gravel underfoot? A pathway planted with flowers, a large-scale lantern, or a pair of tightly clipped potted topiaries will provide a sense of progression. Once inside, the foyer gives you the best opportunity to set the scene. Indulge in a sense of drama and be mindful of proportion. In a soaring space drenched with light, a sinuous contemporary sculpture can be enchanting. But even closer quarters can have their charm: black-and-white tiled floors and a stolid library table, a gilt wood console and glimmering Murano mirror, a streamlined industrial pendant and a fluffy Berber rug. Whatever the mood, the prevailing sentiment should be "Welcome!"

At the Ojai, California, farm of Brooke
and Steve Giannetti, a rose-lined gravel pathway
is an inviting approach.

right: With grass growing through pavers, clipped hedges, and a pedimented front door that offers peeks of ocean views, a house by Mark D. Sikes in Montecito, California, practically embraces visitors. below: The façade of a new house in Birmingham, Alabama, by James Carter feels charmingly timeworn, thanks to whitewashed brick. opposite: A twisting contemporary sculpture by Mark di Suvero is the showstopping centerpiece of a Beverly Hills foyer by Daniel Cuevas.

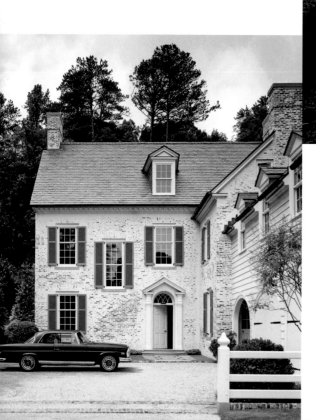

Moorish arches, decorative pagodas, and a riot of pattern and color lead the way to an exotic bathroom at Argyle Farm, the Malibu, California, retreat of Hutton and Ruth Wilkinson.

B *bathtubs*

A bathtub can seem more fantasy than fixture, conjuring the glamorous luxury of a good long soak. But it's arguably the most powerful decorative element in what is essentially a utilitarian space. Its potential for establishing atmosphere and giving the room a graceful sense of occasion is boundless. A claw-foot cast-iron number smack in the center of the room can be a sculptural focal point. Sidle a curvy marble basin up to windows with a gorgeous view and you've created the most sybaritic of escapes. Surrounding a wood-paneled built-in with the kind of cushy upholstered chairs and settees you might otherwise save for a sitting room can transform a heretofore afterthought space into an intimate setting for story time or the coziest of tête-à-têtes. Just add water.

right: In Shawn Henderson's upstate New York house, a vintage claw-foot tub matches plank-paneled walls. below: Pebbled stone floors and lush views provide a glorious sense of place to a Costa Rica bathroom by Beth Webb. opposite: Ceilings and walls of glass give Brooke and Steve Giannetti's Ojai, California, bathroom a verdant garden setting.

A bathtub is the most *powerful decorative element* in what is essentially a utilitarian space.

from left: Cathy Kincaid uses wood paneling, decorative porcelain, and a cushy armchair and bergère to furnish a Dallas bathroom with loads of comfort. / In Colette van den Thillart's Canadian lakeside escape, a niche and plank paneling provide rustic charm.

from left: The bath in an oceanside shingle-style compound by Thomas Kligerman balances sleek proportions with cypress-lined environs. / Sharon Simonaire updated a historic Sag Harbor, New York, space with a serene patina.

left: Matching vintage iron beds and patterned curtains make Suzanne Tucker and Timothy Marks's Montecito guest room feel like a haven. below: In London, Jean-Louis Deniot crafts a mod moment with a vintage starburst mirror and a custom bench. opposite: A gilded corona in a California bedroom by Laurie Steichen was fashioned from a French altar fragment.

beds

If a house is a retreat, then the bed is its innermost haven and its most essential luxury. Romantic types might opt for a tall canopy trimmed in diaphanous curtains, or a blowsy chintz complete with bows and flounces (and an extra emphasis on ceiling height to boot). More subtle is a tufted upholstered headboard in soft velvet or supple linen—all the better to lean against when reading or partaking from a breakfast tray. A wrought-iron tester can have a masculine edge while adding a dollop of patina, whereas nothing says simplicity like a tightly tucked mattress on a platform *à la japonaise*. Above all, don't neglect comfort. A well-made bed is an escape in itself—a down-lined, linen-layered, Egyptian-cotton cocoon. And a good night's sleep is a cure-all that's impossible to beat.

An antique pagoda bed once belonging to Jennie Jerome Churchill (Winston's mum) is the centerpiece of a chinoiserie-inflected room at Hutton and Ruth Wilkinson's Malibu farm.

right: Simple curtains on a canopy mingle with an American quilt and framed toile fragments in Furlow Gatewood's Americus, Georgia, home. below: In a guest room in his Montecito retreat, Richard Hallberg pairs a wrought-iron tester with plenty of texture and white walls. opposite: A crisp leather-clad headboard echoes the pattern on a vintage chest of drawers at Elda and Nicola Fabrizio's Lipari, Italy, escape.

A well-made bed is an escape in itself—a down-lined, linen-layered, Egyptian-cotton cocoon.

In an Atlanta bedroom, Carolyn Malone matches understated elements like plaster walls and plank floors with a theatrical sparkling multitiered chandelier.

chandeliers

What could be more dramatic than a glinting chandelier? A sparkling, crystal-studded lighting option is like a piece of jewelry for the dining room or foyer, creating a beguiling zone of intimacy around the dinner table or casting an alluring glow as you greet and welcome guests. (As a general rule of thumb in a dining room, the bottom of the fixture should hang thirty to thirty-six inches from the top of the table, so there's plenty of space for diners to interact without dodging errant branches of gilt brass and glass.) But don't limit their application to grand or expected spaces. Matched to humble elements, all those swirling tiers and faceted teardrops can be jaw-dropping over a bathtub, or act as an elegant, imaginative foil to plain plastered walls left bare. And over a bed in an otherwise serene neutral room with a minimalist bent? Absolutely breathtaking.

from left: A contemporary chandelier helps unify traditional and modern furnishings in a Montecito sitting room by Ann Holden. / An elaborate, sculptural version in a California kitchen by Laurie Steichen brings drama to a kitchen island.

from left: Greg Stewart of ODADA punctuates a fireside dining area in Carmel, California, with a spectacular fixture. / In Hutton and Ruth Wilkinson's Malibu ranch, a fanciful shell-encrusted model designed by the late Tony Duquette brings whimsy to a guest room with rustic bones.

chandeliers

Though they run an impressive range from floridly traditional to streamlined moderne, what all great chandeliers have in common are branching arms in reflective materials, studded with crystal or glass drops—light-catching qualities that make for spectacular fireworks indoors.

In Veere Grenney's London living room, a measured dose of chintz picks up the hue of sumptuous velvet-lined walls. opposite: A vivid Washington, D.C. living room by Alessandra Branca gets a graceful boost from pops of graphic chintz.

chintz

Its heyday may have been the ball-gown-and-big-hair 1980s, when designers like Mario Buatta lined rooms entirely in plump cabbage roses, but this floral fabric traces its roots to colonial India, and its appeal has spanned centuries, making it a perennial choice for cultivated, genteel rooms that will look as good thirty years from now as they do today. Despite its use in formal spaces, chintz has a charm that leavens acres of gilt. And designers from Sister Parish to Mark Hampton knew that the pattern turns walls and curtains into hanging gardens that bloom all year long, and sofas and armchairs into tufted beds of roses. Lean in and take a deep breath: blossoms are back again.

curtains

With the exception of upholstery, perhaps no other decorative element can say as much about a room as curtains. And they're one of those design sweet spots because they so deliciously combine form and function: On windows of course, they block noise and light and cocoon a room in splendor when the sun goes down. But they can also be hung from a ceiling or archway as portières to create a soft, subtle division between rooms. In terms of style, the sky's the limit. A dowry's worth of gleaming taffeta with a generous, ball-gown puddle can be as enchanting as a nubby linen trimmed in a simple grosgrain ribbon. True team players, they can blend into the background or take a starring role as you see fit.

Amelia Handegan uses a trimmed light linen to create delic ate swags in a South Carolina vacation home. opposite: In a Costa Rican villa by Beth Webb, a breezy floor-to-ceiling pattern matches the tropical setting.

Curtains in a subtle ticking stripe make sleeping loft beds in a Tennessee cabin by Tammy Connor feel extra cozy.

A rustic daybed is the cornerstone of a cozy seating arrangement on the porch of Colette van den Thillart's Canadian cabin.

daybeds

The daybed is a form that reaches back to classical Greece, and it turns out the ancients knew a thing or two about furniture. This is a hardworking, versatile staple. It's indispensable as a room divider, providing ample seating and a subtle delineation that feels lighter, visually speaking, than a sofa—and perhaps no other piece is quite as handy for a cocktail party. It can also function as an anchor in a nook or corner, giving substance to a tight spot while providing a cushy perch. On a purely indulgent level, it's an oasis of comfort: an invitation for curling up with a good book or whiling away an afternoon in a particularly plush, stylistic version of *dolce far niente*.

dining rooms

Despite reports to the contrary, the dining room is alive and well in decorating circles. And there are plenty of good reasons to keep a space strictly dedicated to breaking bread in the house, foremost among them being the ability to maintain a healthy sense of occasion (even if it's just you and a morning bowl of yogurt). All the elements that create a dining room can be distilled into three things: a table, seating, and lighting. But the way you mix up these standard ingredients is limited only by your imagination: Will it be a marble-topped Saarinen table or elegant George III antique? Curvy Thonet chairs or straight-backed Louis XIV? Reflective surfaces, like a mirrored sideboard or walls splashed in a juicy lacquer, will reflect the glow of candlelight and extend the magic.

In a New York room by Alex Papachristidis, gilt chairs mingle with a contemporary table and glinting, scenic custom wallpaper. **opposite:** The dining room of Danielle Rollins's Atlanta house is a mélange of color, pattern, and elegant antiques.

Walls lacquered in a beguiling
shade of baby blue reflect
candlelight and make a
Greenwich, Connecticut,
dining room by Suzanne
Kasler feel magical at night.

door knockers

As the first thing people see when they get to your front step, a knocker sets the mood with panache. It should have some heft and feel heavy in the hand (the better to call your attention to a visitor on the stoop). Think of it as eye candy for your façade—a charming bit of bling that says hello before you even open the door.

The garden at Richard Hallberg's
Montecito escape unfolds as a beguiling
enfilade of outdoor rooms.

Enfilades

The classic enfilade—a series of rooms with doorways aligned along a single axis that affords views from one end of a structure to the other—has its roots in historic palaces like Versailles, where the procession of spaces could be used to denote rank; only the noblest of courtiers would be granted access to the farthest, most intimate sanctums of the king or queen. While no longer a function of royal protocol, an enfilade still bestows a regal kind of grace. It's a fitting showcase for architectural features such as arches, moldings, and vaults, and can be an excellent way of highlighting a fabulous view—there's something enchanting about a front door that offers a peek of crashing waves beyond the backyard. The technique can even extend into the garden, with hedges for walls, gravel for floors, and a lushly framed stone statue in the distance beckoning visitors to walk on.

right: Black-and-white floors and chinoiserie panels provide a sense of progression in a Dallas apartment by Cathy Kincaid. below: In Beverly Hills, Daniel Cuevas uses lanterns and a far-reaching vista to highlight cross vaults. opposite: Arches and a nuanced palette lead the eye to a stairway landing in a Houston house by J. Randall Powers.

An enfilade bestows *a regal grace;* is a fitting showcase for architectural features such as arches, moldings, and vaults; and can be an excellent way of highlighting a fabulous view.

An inset panel of brass rods gives a fireplace in a London bedroom by Jean-Louis Deniot a seductive modernist edge.

Fireplaces

Just because we no longer require hearths to warm our homes and cook our food doesn't mean we no longer *need* them. On the contrary, the primal attraction of a roaring fire is always a boon to a room, especially if the display is framed by a standout mantel. The crowning touch for a traditional living room is a neoclassical fluted and pedimented version in pale and elegant stone. There can also be primitivist beauty in simple slabs of stone set against a clean expanse of creamy plaster. A screen, fire tools, and andirons are accessories that only add to the allure—something nickel plated and sumptuous or wrought iron and rustic? And don't forget to add ample seating for enjoying the show: a tufted leather fender or a circle of furniture in cosseting linens or velvets are pleasant perches to warm your hands when fresh in from the cold.

The primal attraction of a *roaring fire* is always a boon to a room, especially if the display is framed by a standout mantel.

above: In a North Carolina house by Betsy Brown a molding-clad fireplace divides a grand space and shelters a serene seating area. opposite: A surprisingly placed fireplace greets guests in the entryway of an Alabama house by Susan Ferrier, Bobby McAlpine, and Scott Torode.

floors

The most basic of building blocks starts with the surface area under your feet, and it can be the most evocative, atmospheric design choice you ever get to make. Floors are literally and figuratively the foundation that will give everything else in the house a framework. It's important that they provide a sense of place: black-and-white checkered marble in the foyer of a stately Georgian, wide pine planks in a rural farmhouse, unvarnished parquet de Versailles to split the difference between both ends of the spectrum in a country retreat that's refined but also relaxed. A well-placed Oushak or thickly woven seagrass mat can heighten the effect, but there's also something powerful about standout floors in a bold material left completely bare.

In the foyer of a New York apartment, Miles Redd transforms wood flooring with a graphic black and white faux marble paint finish.

above: For a Sag Harbor, New York, dining room, Sharon Simonaire ripped out linoleum to find plain planks that she then varnished with wax for a raw appeal. opposite: In a Maine vacation house by John Saladino, fieldstone floors evoke the rustic setting.

above: Parquet salvaged from a Paris flea market is a grace note in a stair hall by Frank de Biasi on the North Shore of Long Island, New York. opposite: In North Carolina, Betsy Brown uses high-gloss paint as a foil to a rough-spun rug in the same ivory shade.

floor lamps

The floor lamp is the unsung hero of the lighting world. Though the accessory is often overlooked, it synthesizes form and function as few pieces do, providing unobstrusive task lighting in tight spaces where a table might not fit, or casting a soft glow as a focal point, its shapely profile enlivening any room. Do you need something slim and sleek? Strong and sculptural? Utilizing rich materials, ranging from brass to ceramic to leather, there's something to fit the bill no matter what direction you choose.

A collection of Indian art gives a stairwell in Michelle Nussbaumer's Dallas home eye-popping impact.

gallery walls

Here's one of those big decorating secrets to keep under your belt: there's power in numbers. When you group even otherwise forgettable art en masse along an expanse of wall, the collection will suddenly gain the kind of impact each individual piece could never dream of achieving on its own. It works with practically anything—secondhand engravings, silhouettes, black-and-white photography, taxidermy. When hanging, it's helpful to arrange things in a grid that forms a rectangle or a square, being careful to keep an even distance between each work. But don't let an oddly shaped scrap of wall or an incomplete collection stop you—build with what you have in an orderly fashion and the arrangement will still have oomph. If you're going for a polished, pristine look, opt for matching frames to give the installation cohesion. Disparate frames have their own charm, too, with a whimsical, idiosyncratic look that feels amassed over time.

right: In the study of Jan Showers's Dallas townhouse, a grid of engravings match the architectural heft of a pedimented mirror. below: Botanical art by Lauren Lachance gives a New Orleans dining area by Ann Holden visual depth. opposite: A New York hallway by Cathy Kincaid feels elegant with a collection of antique botanical prints.

When you group even forgettable art en masse, *the collection* will suddenly gain the kind of impact each individual piece could never dream of achieving on its own.

In a historic Montecito estate, Ann Holden combines millwork and architectural antiques to give an entry hall a regal grace.

hallways

As transitional spaces meant to move people from one place to the next, hallways, you might think, deserve short shrift. Well, think again. When you consider that these teeny bits of interior real estate can provide a sense of progression while getting you where you need to go, they suddenly become integral to furnishing atmosphere. Consider a grand enfilade with substantial marble architectural details that links the public areas of the house; give it some noble seating options and layer in texture with rugs and fabric and voilà: a design throughway meant to get people from point A to point B is suddenly a place where they might want to linger.

right: The master foyer of a New York apartment by Thomas Pheasant is a soothing composition of marble floors, fabric-paneled walls, and a neutral palette. below: A custom console floats against a serene backdrop of Venetian plaster in a soothing Palm Beach entry hall by Campion Platt. opposite: Nick Olsen animates a New York foyer with metallic geometric wallpaper, shiny lacquer doors, and painted floors.

These teeny bits of interior real estate can provide a *sense of progression* while getting you where you need to go.

In the guest room of her Gstaad, Switzerland, chalet, Michelle Nussbaumer marries a blue-and-white ikat with a riot of different textiles and sober pine paneling.

ikat

A refined textile that's the result of a complex process that's part weaving, part tie-dyeing, ikats burst onto the scene in a major way in the early aughts and show no sign of going anywhere. That's good news for those of us who find charm in the colorful, slightly inexact patterns the textile is known for and think a bit of cross-cultural bohemianism is the apex of chic (and really, who *doesn't*?). Like many patterns with a distinctive stylistic stamp, a little ikat goes a long way—pillows, curtains, table skirts. But then again, our favorite rule in decorating is that there are no rules in decorating: we've seen gutsy rooms done up in head-to-toe ikat that are totally to die for.

ikat

Though only recently resurgent in design circles, ikats are a centuries-old tradition in a variety of cultures around the world, from the Middle East and Southeast Asia to pre-Columbian South America. Fittingly, today's iterations run the gamut from relatively simple stripes to damasks and richly layered geometrics.

In a Dallas sunroom by Cathy Kincaid, traditional architecture gains a bold, au courant edge with geometric patterned tiles and midcentury modern wicker.

juxtaposition

It's true in romance, life, and decorating: opposites attract. The basic law of nature that pulls two contrary objects together also works magic in interiors. Something electric happens when, say, a crisply upholstered and gilt Louis XIV chair is settled on top of thickly woven rush matting. The elegant piece of furniture exalts the humble floor covering, while the rough-hewn floor covering brings the rarified chair gloriously down-to-earth. Juxtaposition is about balance. Every shiny, sleek thing you bring into a room demands a matte, unpolished counterpoint, every refined object a plainspoken match. Pair a gleaming glass-and-nickel cocktail table with a crusty earthenware lamp; a zaftig, plush sofa and a lean, lithe chaise; wrought-iron garden chairs and a luminous lacquered Parsons table.

Shawn Henderson combines farmhouse simplicity with midcentury modern flair in the kitchen of his upstate New York escape.

kitchens

The fact that, in many houses—despite a plethora of well-furnished rooms tailor-made for entertaining—the kitchen is nevertheless where everyone hangs out is a decorating cliché that people are finally embracing with open arms. Today's cooking spaces are being built with more than just making dinner in mind. They are plush, cushy enclaves that compete with living and family rooms for comfort and style, complete with fireplaces, sofas, and blue-chip art; can accommodate crowds for meals at islands, countertops, and monolithic farm tables; and make a centerpiece of the main event (since cooking has unsurprisingly evolved into a spectator sport), all without sacrificing an iota of functionality. It's a fitting, generous approach that only stands to get hotter.

A marbleized kitchen island adds a sophisticated élan to the rustic kitchen at Colette van den Thillart's Canadian lakeside retreat.

from left: In Maine, John Saladino matches the bucolic setting with Douglas fir paneling and elemental stools. /
A butcher-block counter, antique oak floors, and a happy palette soften a Dallas kitchen by Cathy Kincaid.

from left: A potted fig tree and enormous timber rafters are foils in a minimalist Aspen kitchen by Richard Hallberg. / In a Chicago kitchen by Alessandra Branca, a crisp black-and-white palette has a polished effect.

In the kitchen of a grand Long Island estate, David Kleinberg matches stately architecture to a cool color scheme and a painting by Elizabeth Peyton.

For the renovation of a Manhattan family apartment, Celerie Kemble covered dining room walls in a dazzling shade of cornflower-blue lacquer.

lacquer

A room cloaked entirely in rich, luminescent lacquer is one of the decorating world's most impactful special effects. The technique, which requires layer upon layer of painstakingly applied paint, practically drips with glamour. It turns powder rooms into gleaming jewel boxes, dens and studies into urbane bolt-holes, and dining rooms into enchanting staging grounds where flickering candles suddenly transform into dramatic displays of light. All those theatrics, though, aren't just for show. The tactic has its practical benefits, too. By saturating the boundaries of a room in a luminescent sheen, it diffuses its edges, making a space feel bigger and ceiling heights loftier. It also is a great disguise for imperfect or mediocre architecture—especially in deep, inky shades—hiding a multitude of sins in its lustrous, liquid depths.

above: An ink-black lacquered entry hall in Toronto by Jan Showers is a counterpoint to glossy white gallery spaces just beyond its doors. opposite: In Connecticut, Suzanne Kasler clad dining room walls in a glossy turquoise.

left: In Bellport, New York, Thomas O'Brien irreverently hangs art over bookshelves.
below: The book-lined living room in Charlotte Moss's East Hampton, New York, retreat doubles as her private library. opposite: Laurie Steichen uses painted boiserie and herringbone floors to give a California library a gracious patina.

libraries

You don't have to be a bona fide bibliophile to appreciate the way book-lined shelves—and especially a library—can give your home warmth and character. It makes a space feel lived in and loved and offers a peek at your passions. Browsing someone's bookshelves is almost like peering into someone's head; you get an immediate feel for their interests and what might make them tick. A library should be a pleasant place to while away the hours. Make sure there are plenty of cushy places to sit and to put your feet up; a sofa and ottoman or plush armchair are de rigueur. So, too, is ample lighting: a pair of lamps on a console, an adjustable floor lamp, backlit shelves.

living rooms

As the main space for gathering, relaxing, and entertaining, the living room is a multiuse space that must be adaptable and, at the same time, characterful, too. It's the space in your house that guests—and possibly you—will see the most, so it's *the* venue to put your best foot forward. It should say something about your style without sacrificing comfort. Multiple seating arrangements can create intimacy in large spaces, fashioning zones for conversation at a party, but won't feel cavernous when you're home alone. Also, incorporate a useful cadre of ottomans, occasional tables, and side chairs—they can be moved around at a moment's notice to accommodate guests, a glass of wine, or a cup of tea.

A corner banquette in a Chicago apartment by Alessandra Branca cleverly subdivides a larger space and creates a cozy area for conversation. **opposite:** In Los Angeles, Windsor Smith breaks up a soaring space with back-to-back sofas and softens it with rugs and floor-to-ceiling curtains.

Creamy neutrals and animal-print accents mix with vintage and antique furniture to create a soothing atmosphere in Adrienne Vittadini's New York apartment.

A New York bathroom by Miles Redd is entirely clad in marble for a particularly luxe effect.

marble

Once the material of choice for temples, palaces, and statuary, marble still retains a patrician grace. Just a touch of the gorgeously grained, evocatively colored stone gives a space an unmatched elegance and nobility—sumptuous as door or window casings or lovely covering a vanity surface. It's a natural choice for bathrooms and kitchens, and used generously—on walls, backsplashes, counters, floors—it can make a room feel like the most luxurious perch in the world.

right: In an Aspen bathroom Daniel Romualdez designed for Aerin Lauder, softly hued brown marble sets off alpine views. below: A mirror-fronted vanity blends seamlessly with two shades of marble in a London bathroom by Jean-Louis Deniot. opposite: In Atlanta, John Oetgen uses dark marble door casings to heighten the drama of a dining room.

left: With custom mirrored pilasters, walls, and a vanity, a Houston powder room by J. Randall Powers is a stunning statement space. below: Laurie Steichen expands a California hallway with an antique mirror arranged behind a painted console. opposite: In a modern New York high-rise apartment, Nicky Haslam adds luminous glamour with mercury glass–paneled walls and door.

mirrors

It's not surprising that ancient cultures thought mirrors were a trick of sorcery; there's something magical about the way a thin piece of glass can capture so completely whatever crosses its path. Magical, too, is the way a mirror can address myriad design challenges in a room: a lack of light, a lack of space, the need for a little sparkle. In fact, hanging a mirror in a strategic spot in a dark, cramped interior is like installing a window with a stunning view—provided you've had the foresight to beautify whatever it reflects, of course.

right: A concave mirror anchors a California dining area by Suzanne Tucker and Timothy Marks. below: In Thomas Hamel's Sydney residence, a mirrored cabinet extends natural light into the dining room. opposite: Mirrored walls brighten a once-dark New York foyer by Peter Dunham.

In Nancy Braithwaite's Atlanta dining room, oversized nailhead trim marks the boundaries of the room and echoes the shape of drawer pulls on a Shaker cupboard.

nailheads

As embellishments go, nailheads are a classic. Their origins are rustic and utilitarian: they were once used simply to adhere upholstery to a piece of furniture. But what began as practical functionality has since evolved into a metallic design flourish that can feel astonishingly fizzy, light, and exuberant—a far cry from your standard image of a leather chesterfield with scrolling arms trimmed in the distinctive metal dots (not that there's anything wrong with that!). Designers such as Jean Royère and, more recently, Ashley Hicks and Miles Redd have installed nailheads on screens and doors in starburst patterns or to imitate millwork paneling. One of our favorite iterations is Nancy Braithwaite's tongue-in-cheek application in her Atlanta dining room, where a large-scale version of the distinctive circles follows the profile of doors and baseboards.

Mark D. Sikes uses his Los Angeles terrace, surrounded by a twelve-foot-tall ficus hedge and dotted with blue-and-white porcelain, as an extension of the living room.

outdoor rooms

These days, outdoor furniture and accessories have been elevated to the level of their indoor counterparts, with rugs, fabrics, sofas, chairs, and tables in sturdy materials that stand up to the elements (and look all the better for having done so) while still packing all the style and sophistication you'd expect in the living room. So there's even less of an excuse for letting the patio, terrace, or loggia feel like an afterthought. The key to a comfortable and composed plein air space is to treat it like an outdoor room, with hedges for walls, the sky for ceilings, and actual blooms standing in for art.

Wire chairs, a decorative pagoda, and plush fabrics make for a welcoming screened porch by Furlow Gatewood in Americus, Georgia.

Swags and garlands adorn a pretty painted
chest of drawers in a Canadian bedroom
by Colette van den Thillart.

painted furniture

A sunny Italian commode emblazoned with a classical scene; a *très jolie* Provençal armoire embellished with brushstroke blooms; practically anything Gustavian—there is a special place in charm heaven for painted furniture. The truly wonderful thing about this genre of antiques is that they so sweetly combine a casual and approachable style with an eminently elegant attitude, especially when slightly faded or worn over time. They look terrific in bedrooms, where they can leaven a pared-down scheme with an unstudied freshness, or cut the seriousness of a space that tilts too pristine. In hallways, foyers, and living rooms, they can be a smile-inducing way of curating an atmosphere that says "Come on in!"

right: A Gustavian daybed and antique French commodes echo the color scheme of a soothing California bedroom by Ohara Davies-Gaetano. below: In Destin, Florida, Susan Lovelace uses a turquoise-hued German commode in a sunny living room. opposite: A chest designed by the late Tony Duquette in Hutton and Ruth Wilkinson's Malibu ranch was used on the film set of *My Fair Lady.*

The truly *wonderful thing* about painted furniture is that it so sweetly combines a casual and approachable style with an eminently elegant attitude.

passementerie

When it comes to truly unique, inimitable interiors, customization is key. The details count. And despite taking up a relatively small amount of real estate, the little flourishes that distinguish a room—a Greek key trim on plain linen curtains, satin bouillon fringe on a velvet-covered ottoman, a sparkly beaded tape on throw pillows—are worth their weight in gold.

left: Gracefully worn antiques and artfully distressed finishes give a formal dining room in California by Laurie Steichen a casual grace. below: In California's Carmel Valley, Greg Stewart of ODADA uses an antique chest with chipping paint to take the edge off contemporary architecture. opposite: A powder room in a new seaside house by Ohara Davies-Gaetano in Orange County has depth and dimension, thanks to weathered, aged elements.

patina

The Japanese call it *wabi-sabi*, a sensibility that accepts imperfections in objects and materials as the cost of doing business in an unpredictable world and proof of their authenticity. Along similar cultural affinities in France, a well-used antique that shows its age in nicks and dings is lovingly referred to as being *dans son jus*—and is usually a little more costly because of it. When little imperfections are sought after rather than disguised, it allows everything around it to breathe a little easier. So here's a lesson that will serve you well in interiors and in life: forgive the flaws. Embrace chipped paint, scratched finishes, tarnished silver. A room that accepts faults with élan can achieve a soulful kind of beauty that mere impeccability never will.

In a New York apartment by Cathy Kincaid, a large-scale paisley blends seamlessly with a subtle bed canopy and linens. opposite: In her Gstaad chalet, Michelle Nussbaumer uses a single swirling print to joyously elevate sober pine paneling.

pattern

If you think of a well-decorated room as a delicious combination of flavors—like a delectable stew—then paisleys, damasks, toiles, chintzes, and geometrics are the herbs and spices you use to season it. And just as in cooking, complementary flavors will enhance the finished product. The classic way to blend is to focus on coordinating colors: a ticking stripe picks up the pinks in a floral, the ground in a paisley echoes tones in a gingham. You could also go with shape: a swirling crewel mirrors the motif on a painted chest, a geometric riffs on the shape of a wire chair. But honestly, the possibilities are only limited by your imagination. We've seen rooms by masterful designers that use pattern with abandon—and they are still positively scrumptious.

Hutton Wilkinson combines a zoo's worth of animal prints with gold tea paper and geometrically patterned curtains in his Beverly Hills home.

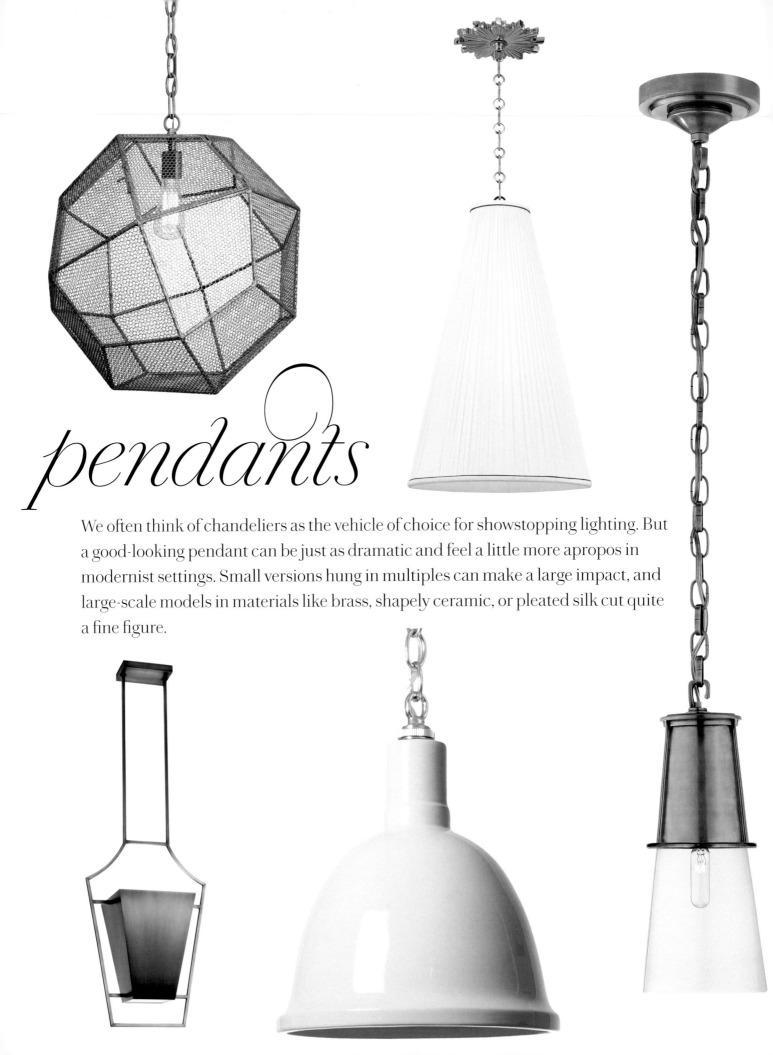

pendants

We often think of chandeliers as the vehicle of choice for showstopping lighting. But a good-looking pendant can be just as dramatic and feel a little more apropos in modernist settings. Small versions hung in multiples can make a large impact, and large-scale models in materials like brass, shapely ceramic, or pleated silk cut quite a fine figure.

133

A tranquil enfilade in a residence by Betsy Brown relies only on a shapely lantern and bench for punctuation.

quiet

Soothing isn't sexy. Subdued, serene spaces often get short shrift when compared to gutsy notice-me interiors that revel in a bounty of color, pattern, and bibelots—especially in magazines, where stunning, statement-making imagery is the bread and butter of the business. But sometimes what you crave most from a room is respite. For many adherents of simplicity, a soft room that makes no demands on the eye is the ultimate antidote to a busy and frenetic work day. And despite appearances, a quiet space is the hardest kind to craft, because when you take away all the bells and whistles, the basics that are left behind are subject to the most intense brand of scrutiny. Subtlety reigns supreme. In the right hands, the results are a soaring, soulful beauty.

above: A restful guest bathroom on Long Island
by Frank de Biasi embraces a subdued palette
and measured doses of pattern. opposite: In
Tara Shaw's New Orleans master bathroom,
patina is the only major stroke.

Lime plaster walls mix with limestone floors, painted Gustavian chairs, and sparkling sconces in Cheryl Skoog Tague's nuanced New York house.

A crisp black range with a graphic tile backsplash is the centerpiece of a polished Beverly Hills kitchen by Daniel Cuevas.

Ranges

If the kitchen is the heart of the house, then the range is its beating center. Increasingly, it can also be the functional space's boldest design statement. Thanks to a variety of bespoke foundries and manufacturers, what used to be a pretty standard choice—stainless steel anyone?—is now available in every shade imaginable, from pink to cerulean to lavender. Add luxe custom details like nickel trim and hardware, a matching hood and cabinetry, and a vivid tile backsplash, and you've got a recipe for true beauty.

romance

A canopy bed. Upholstered walls. Tassel tiebacks. Satins, silks, and velvets in candy-hued pastels. Chintz. Painted antiques. Wicker. Everybody wants to fall in love, and the elements that make up a romantic room are powerfully seductive indeed. They tug on your heartstrings with the promise of pampering and coddling, and you want to sink into them with a sigh. But as with many sumptuous things in life, moderation is essential. Too many frills and flounces and you risk slipping from sweet into saccharine. A successful romantic room is a delicate balance. Curvy Louis XV chairs cry out for a sober metal garden table; if you have acres of ruffles, opt for bare floors. Then step back and let the swooning begin.

In Americus, Georgia, Furlow Gatewood balances a light color scheme and pretty, painted furniture with dark, masculine antiques. opposite: Reclaimed chestnut floorboards ground a plush bedroom in Robert Couturier's Connecticut house.

A vividly patterned rug in a Long Island home by Brian J. McCarthy artfully grounds an ethereal color scheme. **opposite:** In a Montecito house by Christina Rottman a graphic rug matches bold modernist elements.

rugs

They're the canvas you paint a room on, the foundation for everything that comes later, combining texture and tone in a package that's also practical—absorbing and muffling sound and insulating cold floors. Rugs are one of our oldest arts, and its possibilities are literally endless. A gently faded antique Oushak can cloak a space in a gentle wash of color that's a nuanced backdrop for soft palettes. A vivid, graphic Sultanabad can stand up to bolder schemes, while still skewing traditional. More casual striped flat-weave dhurries are classic beach house fare. Contemporary Tibetan silks are a shimmery, sexy counterpart to angular modernist furniture. Fluffy Berbers, sheepskins, or flokatis put tactility front and center, and feel like heaven under bare feet.

In a Marin, California, dining room by
James Huniford, a contemporary striped
rug gives nineteenth-century benches and
a table a fresh new look.

sconces

Originally designed to hold torches along drafty castle walls, sconces have since become a lot more civilized. They're a boon in hallways, illuminating a space where lamps are not always an option. In living rooms, they help layer in light and, with serpentine arms and frills like crystal drops, add a graceful decorative touch. Installed behind the bed in pairs, they facilitate reading late into the night and help provide a sense of harmonious balance. When evaluating sconces, scale should play a major role. A couple of wide sconces with multiple branches are substantial enough to stand up to an antique fireplace and gilt Chippendale mirror, while smaller plaster Art Deco shells might be all you need in a luminous foyer.

right: Vintage French sconces in a Manhattan apartment by Rob Southern are a shapely counterpoint to a contemporary work by John Rosis. below: A delicate mirrored model crowns a mantel in a Washington, D.C. space by Alessandra Branca. opposite: Paul Vincent Wiseman and Brenda Mickel pair delicate brass sconces with an antique mirror in a French-inflected California estate.

In a California home by James Huniford, Italian candelabras are an unexpected foil to a nineteenth-century industrial storage cabinet hung on a family room wall.

In Laurann Claridge's Houston high-rise penthouse, a shapely screen creates a cozy zone of intimacy around a Swedish Empire daybed. **opposite:** Flemish tooled-leather screens function like art along the walls of a guest bedroom in Tom Britt's Water Mill, New York, home.

screens

The folding screen has been enchanting tastemakers for centuries. Invented in ancient China, the decorative tool was quickly adopted around the rest of the globe for its startling utility. This design building block is an attractive way to zone a room, dividing seating areas into smaller spaces to create an inviting intimacy. Highly decorative versions make enticing backdrops for arrangements of furniture. In her day, Coco Chanel owned no less than thirty-two Coromandel screens, which she sometimes used like wallpaper, lining entire rooms with them. Screens can also hide a multitude of sins—uninteresting architecture, a bad view, the luggage you have yet to unpack—all while bringing their own note of color and texture to a space. The added advantage? They have as many personalities as applications.

screens

A shimmering backdrop for a pared-down sofa? A bold dash of color for a corner of the dining room? Pictorial splendor to enliven the study? In a wide-ranging array of materials, from antiqued mirror, to velvet, to parchment and vellum, screens are as bewitching as they are useful. The only thing left for you to do is choose.

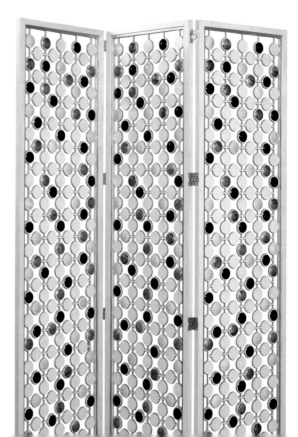

In a monochromatic bedroom by Betsy Brown, sisal rugs play a major decorative role. **opposite**: A sisal rug brings a traditionally inflected, antiques-flecked Chicago living room by Alessandra Branca right down to earth.

sisal

There's a reason you see sisal rugs practically everywhere: they're crisply elegant and casual all at once, and hard-wearing to boot. It's no exaggeration to say they go with literally *anything*—as seamless with Louis XVI bergères and gilt-edged Italian consoles as they are with Art Deco chaises or Barcelona chairs. The fiber itself is woven from the leaves of the *Agave sisalana*, a plant native to Central America, where it has been cultivated since the pre-Columbian era. In modern times, sisal was used mainly for making rope and twine. There is the whiff of that industrial past in the texture of a sisal rug, and also a sense of the tropical—a charming layer of something down-to-earth *and* exotic that's a joy to have underfoot.

In a New York apartment by John Saladino, slipcovered armchairs with dressmaker tabs (a Saladino signature) balance a muscular steel-and-glass table. opposite: A charmingly ruffled, slipcovered sofa in Michelle Nussbaumer's Dallas house brings levity to a serious swirl of antiques.

slipcovers

Back in the Middle Ages, when entire wings of grand estates were left unused for months or even years at a time, furniture was covered in plain muslin that was often tailored to fit each piece to protect upholstery and wooden frames from the elements. By the eighteenth century, the custom was no longer reserved for housekeeping, and for comfort in sultry summers long before the advent of air-conditioning, bons vivants slipped covers of light, breathable fabrics like cotton or linen over armchairs and settees upholstered in formal, heavy damasks or brocades. Many people still switch slipcovers seasonally, of course, and many more adore the breezy, casual feel the accessory can bring to a room all year long. It's kind of like indulging in a little vacation without ever leaving the house.

below: An embellishment of velvet tape gives skirted armchairs in John Saladino's Montecito dining room a surprisingly formal air. opposite: In Costa Rica, Beth Webb provides a dining room with a fitting holiday vibe using elemental slipcovers.

We adore the breezy, *still-on-holiday* feel that slipcovers can bring to a room all year long.

staircases

It's not an accident that some of the most indelible images from classic Hollywood films like *All About Eve* or *Gone with the Wind* involve staircases. Would Bette Davis's or Vivien Leigh's entrances have been half so grand if they'd just popped through a doorway instead of descending a prominent set of stairs? When an architectural necessity can also double as a dramatic design flourish, the resulting alchemy can be breathtaking. The best examples mine a house's spirit—a Georgian-inspired spiral, complete with wrought-iron balustrade; a curvy modernist volume of plaster descending with quiet grace—to provide a sense of rhythm and an apt progression from public to private space.

In Aspen, a bronze-and-glass staircase by Joeb Moore and Victoria Hagan is set against a backdrop of custom oak and offers a series of landings from which to admire a majestic view.

from left: Amelia Handegan matches painted pine floors to Greek Revival splendor in South Carolina. / In Northern California, Paul Vincent Wiseman and Brenda Mickel channel French classicism in florid wrought iron.

from left: Sleek and sculptural minimalist curves by Richard Hallberg help bring a nineteenth-century Boston brownstone gorgeously up-to-date. / For a Spanish Colonial estate in Palm Beach, David Kleinberg recast a stairway in elegant limestone and wrought iron.

above: In a foyer by Betsy Brown, a stairway cast in the same white shades as its surroundings puts emphasis on standout furnishings and accessories. opposite: David Kleinberg updates stately original millwork with cutting-edge contemporary art in a Long Island estate.

In a historic Art Deco Los Angeles house, once owned by Cedric Gibbons and Dolores del Rio, Madeline Stuart lets the glamorous original staircase shine.

symmetry

The simplest formula for furnishing a room with a soothing sense of harmony is to employ symmetry—quite possibly the oldest trick in the book, as a storied succession of architecture and interiors, from the Parthenon to Versailles, amply proves. Balance, it's no great revelation to say, is pleasing to the eye. So flank a fireplace with a pair of sconces or two works of large-scale contemporary art. Match a deep-seated sofa in a capacious living room with another of equal volume. The only caveat? Don't be slavish in your interpretation or your arrangement might fall flat. Fiddle with shape, size, and visual weight—marrying a curvy chaise to a straight-backed but ample armchair, for example, can even out a room without feeling matchy-matchy.

Architecture, sconces, wallpaper, and armchairs conspire to create a harmonious, glimmering Houston bathroom by J. Randall Powers. opposite: In a Greenwich, Connecticut, living room by Suzanne Kasler, a curvy antique recamier is an unexpected counterpoint to a clean-lined Louis XIV–style armchair.

A flocked velvet pillow in Andrew Brown's Birmingham, Alabama, guest room gives a malachite-patterned wallpaper dimension.

T

texture

In many ways, texture is the unsung hero of interior design, the grizzled character actor in an ensemble cast that gets second billing to star players like architecture, art, or antiques with provenance. But make no mistake: the picture would not be the same without him. Whether quietly bringing an exalted suite of gilt-edged furniture discreetly down to earth in the form of nubby linen curtains or a thickly woven seagrass rug, or softening a sleek, pared-down room with cushy velvet or plush chenille, this under-the-radar tool is long overdue for a hearty standing ovation.

above: An Aspen abode by Richard Hallberg marries angular modern furnishings with monolithic raw wood beams and fluffy white rugs.
opposite: In London, plush upholstery, trompe l'oeil wallpaper, and tactile accessories electrify a sitting room by Jean-Louis Deniot.

In a Utah vacation cabin, Anthony Baratta uses backsplash tiles to re-create a quilt-like motif. *opposite:* Floral Portuguese tiles give a crisp blue-and-white bathroom by Mark D. Sikes in Montecito a romantic flair.

tiles

Tiles have paneled high-traffic areas since the beginning of civilization—they're a tried-and-true method for giving kitchens and bathrooms a measure of chic durability. But that doesn't mean they should be limited to those spaces, either. The artisanal sensibility that a hand-painted, color-splashed tile gives a room can be enchanting: a dining room with a chic wainscoting in blue-and-white Delft squares, tumbled and waxed terra-cotta pavers providing warmth in an airy great room, a happy grid of graphic encaustic splendor underfoot in a sunroom. In unconventional applications, though, furnish the space with plenty of soft goods to absorb the sound that will ricochet across all those flat surfaces: plush rugs, ample curtains, and plump upholstery will combat a cacophony.

above: A Costa Rica kitchen by Beth Webb gets a graphic geometric punch from an intricately patterned backsplash. opposite: In an Atlanta dining room by John Oetgen, black-and-white marble is an elegant backdrop.

A headboard, bed curtains, and throw pillows cocoon a French-flavored California bedroom by Anthony Baratta. opposite: An eighteenth-century toile brightens pelmets and curtains in a Connecticut farmhouse remodeled by Kahlil Hamady.

toile

At their inception hundreds of years ago, toiles were made strictly from cotton, printed with wood blocks, and imported to Europe from India. In an age before airplanes, telephones, and Instagram, they were the ultimate status symbol, smacking of wealth and worldliness, and were used not just for sofas and chairs but on waistcoats and ball gowns, too. Competition with native industries eventually led to domestic interpretations in France and England. The merchant Christophe-Philippe Oberkampf spawned a French icon when he founded his factory in Jouy-en-Josas, near Versailles, in 1760. Since then, the distinct allure of toiles has endured the test of time. Undeniably appealing on curtains, walls, and furniture, they lend a healthy dose of romance and grace to any space.

In the living room of a Victorian house in New Jersey, Miles Redd echoes the tone in glossy walls with piping on a custom sofa.

upholstery

Can you imagine a living room without a sofa, a den without an arm-chair, or a bedroom without a chaise? Upholstery is quite possibly the one thing no house can live without. The single most important factor to consider is shape. What kind of profile are you looking for? A scroll-arm or camelback sofa offers something soft and sensual; a deep-seated number with a square silhouette can be just as welcoming, if a little more sleek. Above all, don't skimp. As an ample antiques market proves, quality upholstery can last hundreds of years, and bespoke details like hand-tied springs and sculpted horsehair stuffing are well worth the investment (and amortized over the lifetime of a piece, they are actually quite a value).

above: In a Houston guest room with a quiet scheme and an absence of pattern, Pamela Pierce adds interest with tufts on Napoleon III beds. opposite: Velvet tufts and bullion fringe give an Atlanta sitting room by Melanie Turner a hefty dose of glamour.

Weathered wood and elemental concrete couple with side-mounted faucets to create a sublime vanity in a Florida master bathroom by Rozanne Jackson, Marieanne Khoury-Vogt, and Erik Vogt.

V

vanities

The vanity is one of the bathroom's major design elements. Like little else in the essential space, it defines the room and can also provide valuable storage, a sought-after commodity in especially tight floor plans. Made from materials as varied as chrome and marble or weathered and painted wood, and including details such as carved or curving legs, the right vanity will deliver an incomparable kind of atmosphere, whether you're looking to furnish an elegant powder room or a breezy beach house bathroom where workaday cares simply melt away.

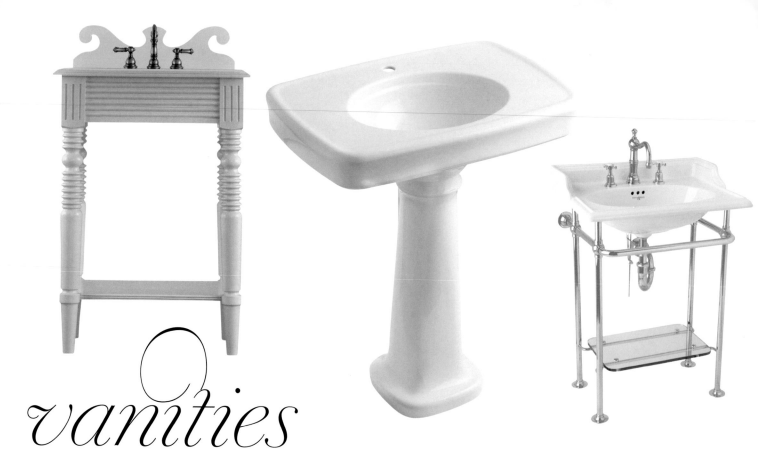

vanities

A good vanity aptly marries form and function. It should have a counter wide enough to handle an array of daily toiletries, deep drawers to keep them hidden and organized when they're not in use, and a ledge or cabinet for keeping towels within arm's reach. The rest—whether you opt for sleek, Deco-inspired sophistication or sculpted wood with the feel of a traditional antique—is completely up to you.

vintage

In the design-magazine world, any accessory or piece of furniture that isn't older than 1900 counts as vintage, not antique. Since that broad designation encompasses everything from sober Edwardian settees to plaster Art Deco torchères to sleek midcentury modern tables, there's no such thing as a single "vintage" look. Suffice it to say that any room, no matter its mood or style, can benefit from an object that has a well-worn, lived-with sensibility (just the mere fact that it's been around so long is a testament to its appeal). There's nothing colder than an interior in which everything is showroom fresh. Since there are so many vintage options from which to choose, there's really no reason your living room should give you the chills, right?

A vintage Maison Jansen dining chair inspired Nick Olsen to create seven custom copies for this New York dining room, which also includes a vintage Serge Roche torchère.

right: In London, Jean-Louis Deniot crafts a mod moment from vintage lamps and pendants and a custom console. below: A vintage chair in disrepair is a sculptural focal point in Quinn Pofahl's and Jaime Jiménez's Southampton, New York, retreat. opposite: In the living room of a London townhouse by Jean-Louis Deniot, a vintage bronze-and-steel cocktail table by Belgian designer Ado Chale is the showstopping centerpiece.

Encompassing everything from sober *Edwardian settees* to plaster Art Deco torchères to sleek midcentury modern tables, there's no such thing as a single "vintage" look.

A large-scale grisaille mural is the major decorative stroke in a Montecito dining room by Ann Holden.

wallcoverings

They can be theatrical and bold, quiet and textural, pretty and charming—or a combination of all of the above. And it's probably the easiest embellishment you can make to a room outside of a good paint job. In materials as diverse as silk, seagrass, and cork—they're no longer just made of paper, so wallpaper is something of a misnomer—a standout wallcovering can be the defining statement in a room: a grisaille mural paneling a refined dining room, a glimmering silk floral bringing glamour to a jewel-box powder room, a small-scale pastel print sweetening a bedroom. On the other hand, wallcoverings can also subtly augment a room with a nuanced backdrop of color and texture: tactile ribbed grass cloth in a library, silvery tea paper on a foyer ceiling, tromp l'oeil stonework lining a hallway.

from left: Wallpaper printed with climbing peonies subtly enhances ceiling heights in a Dallas dining room by Cathy Kincaid. / In a Richmond powder room by Suzanne Kasler, taffeta curtains and trim and diminutive sconce lampshades echo the tones in an enveloping silk wallpaper.

from left: A grisaille mural gives the foyer of a new Chicago triplex by Alessandra Branca a graceful sense of history. / In another Chicago project, Branca used a bird-and-bloom silk wallcovering in a jewel-box powder room.

wicker

In what might be an apocryphal story, the society doyenne and tastemaker Marella Agnelli once remarked after being given a tour of an especially overdecorated home that it would take its owner "another lifetime to understand wicker." Agnelli herself, of course, has long been a devotee, and for good reason: no matter the décor, a room gains something from a touch of wicker. The understated weaving technique (wicker can be wrought in anything from classic rattan to new age synthetics) brings a dose of texture to contemporary spaces and can leaven even the most formal of traditional scenes. It's also a versatile shape-shifter: taking on forms as varied as chairs, lighting, baskets, and mirrors, it's excessively easy—and stylish—to adopt, indoors and out.

A neutral space by Betsy Brown is suddenly sublime with the addition of matching sculptural rattan wicker chairs. opposite: In Atlanta, Kay Douglass uses large-scale wicker pieces as the punctuation in a mostly white sunroom.

wicker

From the most stylish dog bed imaginable to a deliciously unbuttoned starburst mirror to a classic armchair with your porch's name on it, wicker has more personalities than you can shake a stick at. Call it a wonder weave, and embrace its endlessly inventive, easily adaptable, plainspoken charms.

In an Aspen house remodeled by Joeb Moore and Victoria Hagan, a window frames mountain views, and furnishings, like 1940s side chairs and a contemporary console, purposely play a secondary role. opposite: The pièce de résistance of a New England master bedroom by Thomas Kligerman is a floor-to-ceiling window commanding an ocean vista.

windows

Sometimes the most dominant factor in a room isn't inside the room at all. A well-placed window can frame a view that beats any kind of blue-chip artwork, paint job, or treatment, bringing Mother Nature front and center, and needing little else in the way of embellishment. Architecturally speaking, a window bare of muntins will emphasize exterior splendor with unobstructed vistas that also blur the boundaries between indoors and out—particularly heavenly in seaside or mountaintop locales. When the view is secondary to the introduction of light and air, however, structural flourishes like muntins can help provide a sense of progression—making you feel like you're sufficiently sheltered from the elements—and giving larger-than-life windows a delightfully human scale.

above: In Paul Vincent Wiseman's California house, a large-scale daybed furnishes a plush perch overlooking San Francisco Bay. opposite: Steel-framed casement windows with muntins in an Atlanta master bathroom by D. Stanley Dixon and Carolyn Malone have a down-to-earth scale despite an ample footprint.

An X-base table with a strong profile is enough to ground an ethereal monochromatic enfilade in an Arts and Crafts–style house by Betsy Brown.